What's
right?

• • • • • • • • • • • • •

What's
wrong?

What's right?
What's wrong?

A Guide to Talking About Values for Parents *and* Kids

Jeffrey A. Marx *and* Risa Munitz Gruberger

Reader's Digest

The Reader's Digest Association, Inc.
Pleasantville, N.Y./Montreal

Dedication

To our parents:

Robert and Ann Marx
Richard and Judy Munitz
who taught us right from wrong

And to our children:

Michael, Brittney, Sarah,
Jonathan, and Benjamin
to whom we pass this wisdom on

Acknowledgments

Our thanks to all the wonderful people at becker&mayer! who helped make this book possible: Jim Becker; Andy Mayer; Kerry Tessaro; Alison Herschberg, who served as gentle critic and cheerleader *extraordinaire*; and Jennifer Worick, who edited and shepherded the manuscript to completion. Special thanks also to Dr. Jerri Wolfe for her critical reading of the final text.

Finally, our thanks to our children and friends on whom we "tested" the dilemmas; and to the families we have known throughout the years, who shared the real-life dilemmas that appear in this book.

A Reader's Digest Book

What's Right? What's Wrong? is produced by becker&mayer!, Kirkland, Washington
www.beckermayer.com

Design by Amy Redmond
Illustrations by Erik Boucher, Matt Hutnak, Dan Minnick, and Amy Redmond
Edited by Jennifer Worick and Alison Herschberg

Library of Congress Cataloging in Publication Data
Marx, Jeffrey.
    What's right? what's wrong?: a guide to talking about values for
parents and kids / Jeffrey Marx and Risa Munitz Gruberger.
       p. cm.
    ISBN 0-7621-0099-0
    1. Children--Conduct of life--Study and teaching. 2. Values
clarification. 3. Moral education. I. Gruberger, Risa Munitz.
II. Title.
BJ1631.M34 1998
170—dc21   98-38630

Contents

Introduction

There is no job more joyful and difficult than raising a family. Some of our most joyful moments come when our children use good judgment in difficult situations, when a child does not give into peer pressure, or when our children stand up for what is right. Some of our most difficult moments come when we hear our children using inappropriate language to express their anger or refusing to stand up for a sibling in need. While examples of our own honesty, kindness, and respect for others go a long way toward teaching our children morality, they are not enough. Learning what is right and what is wrong requires many conversations in which we, as parents, share our opinions and wisdom with our children while giving them opportunities to solve life's problems.

There are different levels at which parents deal with their children's moral dilemmas. Some parents just shake their heads and wonder why their children are not better behaved; others wait for situations to occur and then use them as learning opportunities. A third approach is to discuss problems *before* they occur. By talking about moral dilemmas with our children before they happen, we provide them with powerful tools for coping with similar problems.

What's Right? What's Wrong? is designed to provide your family with opportunities to discuss some of the tough topics that may come your way. Because we know that discussing value-laden issues is hard, we have developed 67 scenarios to provide a focus for your discussions. Following each scenario is a section titled "Family Discussion." We have provided you with thoughts, concerns, and possible outcomes for each situation. Depending on the ages of your children, you can read aloud the Family Discussion or read the notes first to yourself and then summarize key points in language all family members can understand. This way, parents can think about their own response to the proposed situation and guide the discussion toward what they think is the right ethical solution. Each problem is an opportunity for family members to explore, question, and clarify the moral values they hold.

In constructing these situations, we have relied on the work of two major developmental learning theorists, Jean Piaget and Lawrence Kohlberg. Both Piaget (cognitive development) and Kohlberg (moral development) believed there are distinct, sequential stages children must pass through if they are to reach mature levels of cognition and moral development. Accordingly, the moral situations in this book are presented in a developmental sequence, with those designed to challenge younger children at the beginning of each chapter and those for teens toward the end. Scenarios specific to adolescents are clearly marked "For Teens" in the upper right-hand corner throughout the book. The settings and characters of some scenarios are unique to a particular age; others are appropriate for all ages.

As we began work on the book, we naturally turned to our experiences with our own children, who range in age from three to fifteen. We also referred to our years of experience working with families who came to us for help in resolving problems they were facing, as well as those who wanted to proactively teach their kids about right and wrong, but were not sure how to go about doing so.

What's Right? What's Wrong? can be used while gathered around the kitchen table, relaxing before bedtime, waiting at the doctor's office, sitting on a park bench, or taking a trip in the car. These short, easy-to-understand scenarios are also perfectly suited to family meetings. They can be read out loud and discussed using the questions as a starting point. We hope that this book will create a "learning space" where you and your children can express your opinions, moral values, and wisdom. We invite you to use this book as a guide to inspire you and your family to explore ethical and moral situations we all face on a daily basis.

And there is one more thing: *What's Right? What's Wrong?* is fun. Enjoy laughing together as a family while you work through the dilemmas. When times get tough, remember that communication is the key to your family's growth.

A Birthday Invitation

*J*oe's mom tells him she'll take him to a movie for his birthday and explains that there is room in the car for him to invite two of his friends. After thinking it over, he invites two friends from school. Next door to Joe lives another friend, Kyle, who invited Joe to his birthday party last month. Kyle knows that Joe's birthday is coming up and he asks Joe what he is doing for his birthday.

1. If you were Joe, what would you say to Kyle?

2. If you were Kyle, how would you feel if Joe told you the truth?

3. Is there a way Joe could tell Kyle the truth without hurting his feelings?

4. Have you ever been in a similar situation?

Sometimes people find themselves in a situation where they do not know whether it is better to tell the truth or to lie in order to spare someone's feelings. When you lie to protect another's feelings, it is called a *white lie*. Usually, telling the truth is the best policy. Do you think Kyle's feelings would be hurt if Joe said, "This year I'm not having a big party; I'm going to the movies and I'm taking two friends from school"? Suppose Joe said, "I'm not sure what I'm doing for my birthday yet. I do know that I'm not having a big party this year." Only some of this is true. How do you think Kyle would feel when he later found out about Joe's plans? If Joe and Kyle have been friends for a long time, it may be impossible to give Kyle the news in a way that doesn't hurt his feelings or make him angry. Being honest in a caring way will help.

Joe has some other choices, too, in addition to telling Kyle the truth. Joe could ask his mom if they could figure out a way to bring another friend to the movie; for example, Kyle's mom could drive him to the movie. Joe could ask to celebrate his birthday in a way that could include more friends. Or he might find a way to do something special with Kyle on a different day.

The Yucky Food

Six-year-old Deena and her family have been invited for dinner at their neighbor's house, the Johnsons'. Deena hates the meal. The meat is tough and the vegetables are unfamiliar. "What's the matter, dear?" the neighbor asks. "You haven't eaten your food!"

"That's because it tastes yucky!" says Deena. "I hate it!"

"Deena!" her father says, embarrassed.

"But, Dad," says Deena. "You always tell me to tell the truth!"

1. If you were Deena's father, how would you respond to her remark at the table?

2. Could Deena have expressed her feelings in another way?

3. What is wrong with being honest if the food does taste yucky?

4. Have you ever been in a situation when you were sorry you revealed the whole truth?

{ Family Discussion }

Whether you are six years old or sixty-six years old, it is very uncomfortable to sit down to a meal where the food doesn't taste good. Most adults in this situation would eat a small amount of the food to cover up the problem. Instead of criticizing her for her honest but seemingly rude remark, Deena's father might have said, "Deena, not all families eat the same food. You don't have to eat everything on your plate."

After the family returns home, he could explain, "I know how hard it is to eat food that is different from what you are used to. But saying the food was yucky might have hurt Mrs. Johnson's feelings." In some cases, it is okay to say something that may not be entirely true in order to spare someone's feelings. For example, in situations like this one, you could say, "I'm not very hungry right now."

Manners are a skill and an art that everyone should learn and practice. Before visiting someone's home, it is a good idea to practice some possible situations where these "yucky" issues may arise.

Death of a Pet

*K*aren is taking care of her five-year-old sister, Janet, while their parents are at the movies. As Karen walks by Janet's room, she notices to her shock that Nibbles, Janet's pet hamster, is lying still in the corner of its cage and appears to be dead. Karen knows how much the hamster means to Janet. Because Janet is asleep, Karen decides to wait to figure out what to do.

When her parents come home, Karen tells them the bad news. She suggests that in the morning they tell Janet that Nibbles ran away. Dad thinks they should tell Janet that Nibbles got sick and they had to take him to the doctor. In a few days, they'll tell her that Nibbles died. Mom feels they should tell Janet the truth when she gets up in the morning, instead of letting any time pass.

1. What do you think of everyone's suggestions?

2. If you were Janet, how would you feel if you knew that Nibbles had died?

{ *Family Discussion* }

Sometimes it is best for some people if they are not told the truth right away. For example, if a friend is coping with another problem, or if he or she is sick, more bad news might be overwhelming. There are also times when it is better for others to be told the truth right away. Can you think of some examples? We may delay telling someone the truth not because it's better for that person, but because telling the truth is difficult for *us*. Can you think of a time you delayed telling someone the truth? Did the delay help or hurt?

Parents sometimes lie to their children as a way of protecting them from sadness. Learning how to cope with sad feelings is an important part of growing up. Death is hard to understand at all ages, but we have to realize that all living things die, including pets. There may not be one right way of explaining that a pet has died. What is most important in this case is allowing Janet to express her feelings of sadness and loss.

The Forgotten Fish

*T*oby's next-door neighbor, Mr. Ferguson, has a fantastic fish collection. Toby loves to go next-door and watch the fish. When he learns Mr. Ferguson is going away for vacation, Toby begs him to let him take care of the fish. Mr. Ferguson is reluctant because the fish have to be fed on a strict schedule. But Toby convinces Mr. Ferguson that he is old enough to do the job and that he will take really good care of the fish. Mr. Ferguson is a little worried about it, but he trusts Toby and agrees to give him this job.

For the first three days, Toby feeds the fish exactly when he is supposed to. On the fourth day, however, he forgets. The next day, when Toby goes into Mr. Ferguson's house, he finds that one of the Siamese fighting fish has died. Mr. Ferguson is due back in two days.

1. If you were Toby, what would you do?

2. If you were Mr. Ferguson, what would you say when you discovered one of your fish had died?

3. How old do you think a person should be to take care of someone else's pet?

4. If you were Mr. Ferguson, would you let Toby have a second chance to take care of the fish?

{ Family Discussion }

Though the missed feeding might be to blame for the death of the fish, another reason may exist. The fish might have died from an illness that can be passed on in the water. If it did, then other fish may be affected. If Toby replaces the dead fish and says nothing, other fish may die. Thus, it is probably best to tell Mr. Ferguson what really happened.

Telling the truth is not always easy. No doubt about it, Toby is going to have a hard time taking responsibility and telling Mr. Ferguson what happened. He will need to think carefully about how to apologize for missing the feeding. He might offer to pay Mr. Ferguson for a new fish or clean his fish tank for a month. Toby should discuss with his parents exactly what to say. Most people realize that it's hard to admit to a mistake, and this usually makes people gracious when they receive an apology.

Skipping School

*F*riday was Daniel's birthday. Even though Friday was a school day and there was a vocabulary test, his parents decided this was the best day to go to his favorite amusement park because it would not be crowded. They decided it would be okay for him to miss school.

Daniel had a wonderful time—it was his best birthday ever! "Remember," his mom said, "When you return to school on Monday, just tell the teacher you were sick."

On Monday morning, Daniel's teacher said, "Daniel, we missed you on Friday, especially since there was a big vocabulary test. Is everything okay?"

1. What might Daniel have said to his parents when they first asked him to lie?

2. If you were Daniel, what would you say to your teacher on Monday?

3. What do you think about what Daniel's parents did?

4. What do you think would happen if Daniel told his teacher the truth?

{ Family Discussion }

It was not fair for Daniel's parents to ask him to lie to his teacher. Daniel is being put between his teacher and his parents in this situation. This is a very awkward position. He could lie. What if his teacher found out? What do you think would happen? Daniel can talk with his teacher privately and explain what really happened. Or he can ask his teacher to talk with his mom.

At times, telling a lie seems like a reasonable, quick solution to a problem. But by asking Daniel to lie, his parents are not taking responsibility for their decision. Even though it was Daniel's birthday, it was his parents' decision to take him out of school for the day. Daniel's parents should consider the long-term effects of asking Daniel to lie. Children learn from their parents. What is Daniel learning in this situation?

Telling on a Friend

*S*chool is over for the day, and the custodian is cleaning the classrooms. Brenda and Mary, who are good friends, are jumping on the custodian's electric cart. On the front seat, they see the custodian's keys, which open every door in school. The girls continue goofing around until the custodian notices and yells at them to leave.

The next morning, Brenda is summoned to the principal's office. The principal tells her someone took a set of school keys that were on the custodian's cart. The custodian remembered that Brenda had been hanging around the hallways after school. Brenda is told that she will be suspended immediately unless the keys are returned. Brenda didn't take the keys, but she wonders if Mary took them.

1. If you were Brenda, what would you say to the principal?

2. Does Brenda have an obligation to report Mary?

3. Is loyalty to a friend more important than revealing the truth?

{ *Family Discussion* }

Brenda could lie and say that she never saw the keys and doesn't have them, but that would be wrong. If Mary took the keys, it could lead to a serious problem. If something is missing and it turns out that Mary is the one with the keys, she is going to be blamed for the theft.

Loyalty is a big part of friendship, but this situation involves an illegal act. If Brenda isn't ready to tell what really happened, she could stall for time and speak to Mary first. It can be difficult to distinguish between covering for a friend and doing something illegal.

In this case, Brenda shouldn't risk getting blamed for something she didn't do. If it comes down to telling on Mary or taking responsibility for the loss of the keys, Brenda needs to tell the truth. Brenda should tell Mary what happened and tell the principal what she knows. But she should be careful not to jump to conclusions about whether Mary took the keys. Hopefully, neither she nor Mary will be judged, except on the facts available.

A Baby-sitting Problem

*T*he Greens are looking for a regular Saturday-night baby-sitter. They decide to call on their neighbor, Rebecca. This baby-sitting job means a lot to her, because she is trying to save money to buy a pair of skis.

After the Greens leave for the evening, their kids get out of control. The whole night Rebecca tries to calm down the children. They don't listen, they talk back to her, and they stay up forty-five minutes past their bedtime. When the Greens come home, Mrs. Green asks, "How were the kids?"

1. If you were Rebecca, how would you answer?

2. Is there a way Rebecca can tactfully tell the truth?

3. If you were Mrs. Green, how would you react if Rebecca told you that your kids weren't well-behaved?

4. Can you think of a time that you told the truth and you lost out on something because of it?

{ *Family Discussion* }

If Rebecca tells the truth, the Greens may think she is unable to handle their kids and won't ask her to baby-sit again. On the other hand, if she tells the truth, perhaps they will respect her because she was honest. Rebecca should tell the Greens that not everything went well, because to say otherwise would be lying.

Rebecca needs to decide if she is really interested in baby-sitting the Greens' children. If she is, then she will need to talk with the Greens about the events of the evening. She should avoid using words like "brat" and "awful" and instead describe in specific terms what happened. For example, she could say, "When I said it was bedtime, Michael refused to go into the bathroom and brush his teeth." Rebecca could explain that it would help her if the Greens would share some ideas on handling the children. She could add that she hopes that as she gets to know the children and they her, their evenings will become easier and fun. Sometimes "softening" the truth avoids confrontations.

Crushed

*A*lissa and Clara are best friends. When Clara sees Alissa talking to Billy, the cutest guy in their class, she can't believe it. Clara has a huge crush on him, and wants to know all of the details of their conversation.

"I saw you talking to Billy in the hallway after history class," says Clara. "Did he say anything about me?" Actually, Billy told Alissa that he couldn't stand Clara, and that he thought she looked like a Martian. Alissa doesn't want to hurt Clara's feelings.

1. If you were Alissa, would you tell Clara what Billy really said about her?

2. Can Alissa tell the truth and still spare Clara's feelings? How?

3. Do you think it is okay not to always tell the whole truth?

4. Have you ever been hurt by hearing the truth?

{ Family Discussion }

If Alissa decides not to tell Clara what Billy said, it might make things worse for Clara in the future. There are tactful ways Alissa could tell Clara *part* of the truth. Remember, the girls are close friends, and Alissa is trying to avoid hurting Clara's feelings. Perhaps she could say something like, "I think Billy knows you're interested in him, but I don't think he feels the same way."

Sometimes it is better to make the truth less hurtful by telling some, but not all of it. Rather than lie and say nothing or tell Clara Billy's hurtful remarks, Alissa could share enough of the conversation to make it clear to Clara that Billy was not interested in her. Sometimes it's better to leave a few details out when telling the truth to another person.

The New Dress

*M*elissa can't wait for Kelly to come over to her house. She is going to show her the new outfit she bought for the school dance. Melissa tells Kelly that she's going to love the dress—it looks like it's straight out of a fashion magazine!

After school, the girls go back to Melissa's house and dash up to her room. Melissa excitedly puts on the dress to show Kelly. When Melissa turns around and asks Kelly what she thinks, Kelly is shocked. She thinks the dress is ugly and unflattering.

1. If you were Kelly, what would you say to Melissa?

2. Should it matter to Melissa what Kelly thinks?

3. If Kelly is a good friend, shouldn't she tell Melissa that the dress is ugly so she won't be embarrassed at the dance?

{ *Family Discussion* }

Melissa loves her dress and is excited to show it to Kelly. Even though she asks Kelly what she thinks, Melissa may really only want to share her excitement. Do you think she really wants Kelly's opinion? Before Kelly answers, she should consider whether her dislike of the dress has to do with differences in "taste" or if there is something really wrong with the dress.

Sometimes people tell a *white lie*, or partial truth, to spare another's feelings. But other times we have an obligation to tell others the whole truth even when we know their feelings will be hurt. Sometimes knowing the truth prevents a bigger hurt in the future. Kelly will need to think about the potential consequences of her response to Melissa's question.

There are ways to be truthful and sensitive at the same time. Kelly could say, "Melissa, I actually don't like the dress very much. We have always told each other the truth about everything. I hope you understand when I say I think a different dress would be more flattering."

The Bad Words

*S*teve and his five-year-old son, Kevin, are driving home from baseball practice. As they stop at a red traffic light, a sports car speeds past them, ignoring the light and almost causing a terrible accident.

"You stupid idiot!" Steve yells. As they continue their drive home, Steve is startled to hear Kevin say, "You stupid idiot!" from the back seat, each time a car passed.

1. If you were Steve, what would you say to Kevin?

2. Is it okay to swear or use bad words? When? With whom? Where?

3. What else could Steve have done when he saw the other driver breaking the law?

4. Can you think of a time when you were really mad at someone and used bad words?

{ Family Discussion }

Words are powerful. They can uplift, support, and encourage others. Words can also put down, discourage, and shame. Calling someone a bad name can have the same effect as hitting a person: hitting causes physical pain, and yelling at someone can cause emotional pain. Kind words are also very powerful. Saying "I love you" can be like giving someone a hug. It is important to think about the words you use before you say them.

Some words are appropriate for certain times and places, and others are not. For example, certain nicknames are okay to use in our homes, but may be embarrassing when used in public. Some words are better kept for use with friends—not with teachers or parents. Sometimes, especially when we are angry, we tend to use words without thinking. Steve's words were caused by his anger at the other driver who almost hit his car.

Acceptable words need to be substituted for those that are clearly not acceptable. For example: "I can't believe you did this! I'm really angry at what just happened! Go away! I can't talk to you right now." Each family needs to decide which words are appropriate when expressing anger. What words or phrases are okay in your family?

The Favorite

*T*odd's parents are out of town for the week, and Grandpa Joe is staying with him at his house. Todd is used to spending more time with his other grandparents, Nana and Papa. He had hoped they would come and stay with him while his parents were away, but Nana and Papa were not available.

One night before bedtime, Todd says to Grandpa Joe, "I don't want you to put me to bed. I want Nana and Papa, and I'm not going to go to bed until they come!" His grandpa is surprised and his feelings are hurt. He decides to call Todd's parents and explain what has happened. Todd comes to the phone and starts to cry.

1. If you were Todd's parents, what would you say to Todd? What would you say to Grandpa Joe?

2. What could Grandpa Joe have done besides calling Todd's parents?

3. What else could Todd have said to Grandpa Joe when it was time for bed?

4. Do you have different feelings about your grandparents or other relatives?

{ Family Discussion }

Relationships between family members are not always equal. It is okay to feel differently about certain family members than you do about others. It is normal to like some people better than you do others, but it is also hurtful to tell someone that he or she is not as special as somebody else. Clearly, Grandpa Joe was hurt by Todd's remark. We all want to be liked and loved by others. That is why most people do not like to hear that you like someone else better than them. Even though Todd was being honest, his honesty might have been best kept to himself.

Special relationships take time to develop. Grandpa Joe can acknowledge Todd's feelings for his other grandparents by saying, "I know you've had a lot of time to do special things with Nana and Papa and I know you miss them. I'm hoping that we can get to know each other better during my visit. Tell me, what are your favorite things to do?" Over the next few days, Grandpa Joe and Todd can do some of their favorite activities together to build a closer relationship.

The Spanking

*W*hen the Baxters return home from an evening out, they are greeted at their door by Mrs. Harris, the baby-sitter. "It didn't go very well tonight at all," says Mrs. Harris. "When I told Liz and Tony they had to go to bed, they refused to listen to me. They went into Liz's room, locked the door, and have been in there for hours."

While Mr. Baxter drives Mrs. Harris home, Mrs. Baxter goes into Liz's room to talk to her children. "She smacked me on my butt when I wouldn't go to bed!" cries Liz. "I got scared she was going to hurt us, so we tried to sneak out of the house and go to the Watsons' next-door. But she came and grabbed my arm really hard! I locked the door so she couldn't get into my room!"

1. If you were Liz's parents, what would you do?

2. If you were Mrs. Harris, how might you have handled the situation differently?

3. If you were one of the kids, what would you have done if Mrs. Harris spanked you?

4. Do you know where to go for safety if you feel threatened?

{ *Family Discussion* }

No matter how angry we get with someone else, it is not okay to hurt them. It is especially terrible for an adult to hit a child. Teachers are not permitted to hit students, coaches are not allowed to hit players, and the same rule applies to other adults. Business owners cannot hit the people who work for them, nor can the workers hit their bosses. If someone hits your car in a parking lot, you may be angry with that person, but you can't hit him or her back. It is against the law.

Regardless of how badly the children were behaving, Mrs. Harris lost control and acted inappropriately. There were other things she could have done to make the children behave, like not letting them have dessert or not allowing them to watch a television program. Mrs. Harris did the wrong thing. What Liz did was the right thing to do if she was scared.

It is important for you to know that you should tell your parents immediately if you have been treated inappropriately or are frightened for your safety. Talk with your family about what you could do in a situation like this one.

Revenge

*M*aria is really angry with her younger brother, Ricardo. He not only went into her room without her permission but took some of her stickers, too.

"Maria," says her mother, "Ricardo's birthday is coming up in two weeks. Do you know what he wants?" Maria knows Ricardo really wants a train set, but she's still angry with him for going into her room.

1. Should Maria tell her mother what Ricardo wants?

2. Should Maria say nothing?

3. Should she make up something awful?

4. Can you think of a time when you stayed mad at someone for a long time?

{ *Family Discussion* }

It is hard to forget when someone has hurt us. When we carry around that hurt, it is called *carrying a grudge.* Sometimes it is hard to let it go. Even if we tell the person that we are angry, and even if he or she apologizes, sometimes we stay mad for a long time.

Some people hold on to their grudges for years and never forget the hurt they received, the contest they lost, being embarrassed in front of others, or being left out. Sometimes life presents us with the opportunity to "get even." This is called *revenge.* Revenge keeps the hurt alive. Sometimes we seek revenge by making up lies about people who hurt us, or we try to do the same thing to them. Revenge leads to more revenge until one person steps out of the cycle.

Learning how to express anger in a constructive way can help you eventually let go of your hurt. There are healthy ways to release anger, such as writing down how you feel, talking about why you're mad, or telling the person who hurt you how you feel.

Grandpa's Accident

*O*scar and Grandpa are carrying a box of groceries together from the car. Suddenly Grandpa loses his footing on the steps and the box tips over, spilling groceries down the stairs. Oscar's mom comes running. "What happened here?" she cries.

"Oh, we just tripped and had a little accident," says Grandpa. Oscar looks at his Grandpa and blinks. He knows it wasn't his fault that the groceries were dropped.

1. What do you think about what Grandpa said?

2. What would you say if you were Oscar?

3. Can you think of examples of how we can show consideration for older people?

4. What does it mean to "respect your elders"?

{ *Family Discussion* }

Grandpa had an accident. He should have taken responsibility for tripping and dropping the groceries. And yet, sometimes it is not necessary to focus on who is to blame. When toddlers who are beginning to drink from a cup accidentally spill it, we try not to yell at them, because we understand that they can't help it. Older people—who may not be as strong or steady as they once were—need our understanding as well. This is why we give our seats on buses to older people or open doors for them. We can also help them up from chairs or offer them an arm to lean on.

In this situation, it would be embarrassing for Grandpa if Oscar said, "I didn't trip, it was Grandpa." The truth is that it was an accident. To blame another is not always important. It may be more important to be sensitive to someone's feelings or situation.

Family Time

Karen is a talented gymnast. She does very well at gymnastic competitions. But she feels she cannot perform as well when her father comes to watch her compete. It's not that he puts any pressure on her—he enjoys watching her perform and is proud of her, no matter whether she wins or loses. Nevertheless, she is self-conscious when he's there.

"Dad," says Karen, "I really can't perform well when you come to see me. I don't want you coming to my meets anymore."

Karen's father is upset. Since he works long hours at the office during the week, his only real chance to spend time with Karen is on the weekends. He loves going to the meets. He asks Karen, "Isn't being together with your family more important than winning?"

1. Is it fair for Karen to ask her father not to come to the meets?

2. If you were Karen, how would you respond to what her father said?

3. If you were Karen's father, what would you do about her request?

4. Is it more important for Karen to do well or for her father to see her compete?

38

{ Family Discussion }

Karen and her father can decide to compromise. Maybe he could come to every other meet. Or Karen could ask her coach for ways to work on concentration so she could stay more focused when her father is at the meet. Compromise should always be considered when there is conflict. When two people compromise, it shows a willingness to meet someone halfway. You don't necessarily get what you want, but you end the conflict and make your relationship stronger.

Doing things together as a family is important, like eating meals, celebrating holidays, going to temple or church, watching television and doing household chores. Talk with your parents about some activities that they did with their families when they were growing up. Sometimes being together as a family is a drag, and sometimes it is fun, but it is important for the whole family to spend time together.

Putting a Pet to Sleep

*S*kippy, a golden retriever, has been a part of the Stern family ever since their kids were born. But now she is old, unable to walk, and is losing her eyesight. Their veterinarian has recommended that Skippy be "put to sleep," instead of dying a natural death.

Dad calls a family meeting to discuss the situation. He suggests they do what the veterinarian thinks is best. Tim is very upset about the idea of killing Skippy. His older brother, Bruce, tells him to grow up and points out that Skippy is just a dog. Mom reminds the boys that Skippy is now in a lot of pain.

1. What do you think the family should do about Skippy?

2. Is there anything else the family could do?

3. What do you think of Bruce's comment to Tim?

{ Family Discussion }

Out of respect and love for Skippy, the Stern family wants to make a thoughtful decision about what is right for her. This means that she should not be killed casually, and it also means she should not be left to suffer. Some animals are kept alive and continue to live in pain. The issue here is not how to avoid Skippy's death, but rather, how long to postpone it.

There is no simple answer to this dilemma. Some people feel that putting a pet "to sleep" is wrong. They believe we should let nature take its course. When a pet is ready to die, he or she will die, but in the meantime, the family members should do all they can to make the pet comfortable. Other people feel that a life of pain is not a life worth living. A family discussion on death, dying, and loss might help the Stern family clarify their feelings about what to do in this situation. As they talk about what to do with Skippy, the family also needs to respect each other's feelings on this sensitive subject.

The Stepparent

*B*ob, Johnny's new stepfather, notices that Johnny is watching television instead of doing his math. Bob asks Johnny to turn off the TV and finish his work. Johnny replies that he wants to finish watching the show. Then he tells Bob that he is not his dad—or his boss—just because he married his mother.

Bob walks over to the television, shuts it off, and tells Johnny to get going.

1. If you were Johnny, what would you do when Bob turned off the TV?

2. What do you think about what Johnny said to Bob?

3. Is it fair for Bob to tell Johnny what to do?

4. If you were Johnny's mom, what would you say to Johnny and Bob?

{ *Family Discussion* }

Families are very complicated, no matter what shape they come in. It is especially hard on families when parents are separated or divorced. It is sometimes more difficult when one of the parents remarries. In that situation, there is a whole new person to get used to, especially when that person is acting like another parent.

Whether the adult in our home is our biological parent or our stepparent, he or she is worthy of respect. We should always treat others with respect—especially adults. Teachers, librarians, and coaches may not be our parents, but they are "in charge" and deserve our respect.

Adults have responsibility to children as well. They can't mistreat children, and need to show them respect. Bob and Johnny are both guilty of not respecting one another. Johnny probably knew he shouldn't have been watching TV before he finished his homework, and what he said to Bob was meant only to hurt his feelings. And Bob should not have turned the TV off without first talking about it with Johnny. In the future, whenever Johnny and Bob have a conflict, they should try to remember that, at times, it's not easy for either one of them to get used to a new family.

Teasing a Friend

*A*lfonso and Jaime have been friends since kindergarten. Now that the boys are in junior high, Jaime has been acting differently. As long as they are by themselves, Jaime's behavior is fine. But when they get around the other guys, Jaime always makes fun of Alfonso and puts him down.

Alfonso is really hurt by Jaime's words. When he tells Jaime to cut it out, Jaime wants to know why Alfonso can't take a little teasing. Alfonso doesn't want to lose Jaime as a friend, but he also doesn't want this situation to continue.

1. If you were Alfonso, what would you do?

2. If you were Jaime, how would you react to Alfonso's complaint?

3. Is it fair for Alfonso to expect Jaime to act a certain way?

4. Have you ever told someone to stop doing something that annoyed or hurt you, and he didn't listen?

{ Family Discussion }

Words can hurt, even if they are just "teasing" or said in fun. When someone tells you that he or she is hurt by your words, even if you think he or she is being overly sensitive, the right thing to do is to apologize and stop saying harmful things. A good friend is someone who knows not only what you do like, but what you don't like. To be a good friend is to treat someone else as you would want to be treated.

Alfonso needs to think about whether or not he still wants to be friends with Jaime. Even though he doesn't want to lose Jaime as a friend, Alfonso needs to learn that people change over time and sometimes friendships change.

The Love Letter

*I*n the hallway at school, Dani discovers a note on the floor. It is a love letter from Kiko to a boy in their class. Dani invites Megan, a good friend of Kiko, to come over after school, and shares the love letter with her. Dani says they should make copies of the letter on a photocopier and hand them out at school.

Megan has wanted to be friends with Dani all year and she is thrilled that she's been invited to Dani's home. If she decides to go along with Dani's idea, she will probably hurt Kiko's feelings and lose her friendship.

1. What would you do if you found a letter like Kiko's?

2. If you were Megan, would you go along with Dani's plan?

3. If she decides not to go along with Dani's idea, does Megan have an obligation to tell Kiko what is about to happen, or should she stay out of the whole situation?

{ Family Discussion }

Some things in our lives are private, such as a diary, drawings, sentimental objects, personal poetry, and family pictures. A letter that is not addressed to you, even if it is not sealed in an envelope, is someone else's private mail. Love letters are *extremely* personal. Kiko would not want her private words shared with others. Dani could have ignored the letter altogether, or read it and then returned it to Kiko, but her plan to make copies of the letter is mean and insensitive.

It may be hard for Megan to say that she thinks Dani's plan to copy the letter is wrong. She will have to decide if her new friendship with Dani is worth hurting Kiko. Thinking about how she would feel if the letter had been hers should help Megan know that she should not go along with Dani's plan.

Embarrassing a Guest

*L*ynn's thirteenth birthday party has finally arrived. She has been talking about this party for weeks. All of her guests gather around her as she opens the presents.

When she opens Elena's present, Lynn yells out, "Who would ever wear this? Thanks *a lot,* Elena." All the girls burst into laughter and Elena is both mad and embarrassed. She spent a lot of time picking out the sweater for Lynn, and what Lynn said really hurt her feelings, especially in front of all their friends.

1. If you were Lynn and opened a present you didn't really like, how would you handle the situation?

2. If you were Elena, how would you react to what Lynn did?

3. If Elena feels that she must say something immediately, what could she say that would be appropriate?

{ Family Discussion }

It is important to stop and consider the time and the place when we are about to express our feelings. In this situation, Lynn blurted out what she was thinking before she considered what might happen. Elena can hold her feelings in, or she can express them right away, like Lynn did.

Sometimes it is a good idea to keep from expressing your feelings until you can really think about what you want to say. Certainly, at some point, we should express how we feel if something is bothering us. Sometimes hurt feelings can grow into anger if they are never expressed. They can churn around inside of us, making us miserable.

Elena has some options. She could get up and leave; she could ask to have a private word with Lynn later during the party; she could write Lynn a note or call her when she gets home. It is usually more effective to share our feelings with someone in private rather than in front of a group of people. This way only the people involved are part of the discussion.

An Unexpected Valentine

*J*udy sits at home, reading the stack of valentines she's received at school. One of them contains rose petals and a handwritten love poem. To her surprise, it's from Catherine, a girl in her class who has always been quite friendly!

Judy shows the valentine to her mom. "What should I do, Mom,?" Judy asks. "I'm not gay! Why would she think I'd be interested? I like Catherine as a friend, not as a *girlfriend!*" Judy knows that this could be very awkward if people at school found out about the valentine.

1. What do you think about the valentine Catherine sent?

2. Should Judy's response be different if the card is from a boy that she isn't interested in?

3. Have you ever had to tell someone that you weren't interested in being in a romantic relationship?

4. If you were Judy, what would you do?

{ Family Discussion }

As we get older, there will be people in our lives, male and female, who will be attracted to us. Sometimes it's because of the interest we show in them, sometimes it's because of the special people that we are. We, in turn, will be interested in spending time with some of them, and even dating them. There will also be people whom we will not want to spend time with or date. While many people in the world are attracted to members of the opposite sex, there are also people who are attracted to members of the same sex. Some people are equally attracted to both sexes.

Whether a situation like this involves someone of the same sex or the opposite sex, the same rules of decency and kindness apply, whether you are interested in the person or not. Perhaps Judy could tell Catherine that she likes her as a friend, but has no interest in dating girls. Or it might be easier for Judy to write Catherine a note instead of saying it face-to-face.

It's very hard to be a young person who has strong feelings for someone of the same sex. Often, he or she is called names or is beaten up. An adult may even lose a job. It is very brave of Catherine to share her feelings with Judy, and Judy should respect her trust and keep her secret.

The Secret Date

*K*aren and Jarrad have been dating each other exclusively for the past six months.

This weekend, while Karen is away, Jarrad calls a girl on the phone. He knows she has a crush on him, and she knows that Jarrad has a girlfriend. Jarrad asks her to go on a date on Saturday night. When she asks if Karen will mind, Jarrad says, "I won't tell if you don't!"

1. What do you think about what Jarrad is doing?

2. If you were Karen, what would be your response if you found out?

3. What would you say to Jarrad if you were the other girl?

4. When people are dating each other exclusively, what obligations do they have to each other?

{ Family Discussion }

Jarrad and Karen have promised one another they will not date anyone else. When two people make such a commitment to each other, they trust that each of them will keep that promise. It is quite clear that if Jarrad goes out with the girl he has called, he is cheating on Karen.

An exclusive relationship is one that is precious and unique. It is not meant to be shared with others. If Jarrad goes out with another girl, his relationship with Karen is no longer just between two people—now there is a third person involved. Jarrad needs to consider how his decision to date someone else will affect Karen. She will undoubtedly be very upset by this news. Before Jarrad makes a date with someone else, he needs to talk about it with Karen. It might be hard for Jarrad to tell Karen he wants to date other people, but she will at least not be surprised when he does so. To cheat on Karen doubles her hurt by showing a lack of consideration for her feelings.

The Broken Vase

*I*t is Friday afternoon, and Marco's mom is shopping for a last-minute wedding present in a fancy store filled with plates, glasses, and other breakable things. She has brought Marco, her young son, with her. As they enter the gift shop, Marco's mom crouches down, looks him straight in the eye, and says, "Now Marco, remember, don't touch anything!"

A few minutes later, as she is looking at items on the other side of the store, she hears a crash. Whirling around, she sees Marco standing at the end of the aisle next to the broken pieces of a vase, shattered on the floor.

"I'm sorry, Mommy," Marco cries. "I bumped against the table!"

"I'm sorry, too, madame," the store owner says to her, "but you will have to pay for that vase."

"But Mommy," cries Marco, "it was an accident! I didn't mean to!"

1. Do you think it's fair that Marco's mom will have to pay for the vase?

2. Was it fair to expect Marco not to touch anything?

3. If you were Marco's mom, what would you do?

{ Family Discussion }

Reminding Marco not to touch something was not enough when his mother took him into a shop with breakable items. She needed to have him close to her, so that she could better ensure an accident wouldn't happen. The store has a rule: Customers must pay if something is damaged or broken. If the store sticks to its rule, Marco's mom must pay for the vase—even if it was broken by accident.

Many times, a person is responsible for an accident: you hit a ball that breaks a neighbor's window; you borrow your friend's toy and it breaks. When an accident occurs and it's your fault, you are responsible for repairing the damage: a new window gets paid for, the toy replaced.

Marco should share the responsibility. He can tell the clerk and his mom that he is sorry. This is sometimes hard to do. If we find ourselves in a situation like Marco's and are shy about saying, "I'm sorry," we can draw a picture or send a letter. Apologizing is important, because we all make mistakes sometimes.

"It's Not My Fault"

*a*fter school each day, Zack stands with the other kids behind a painted white line while waiting for his school bus. One afternoon he is waiting there when Steve, a boy who is always getting into trouble, pushs Zack so hard that he falls over the line. The teacher immediately scolds Zack in front of the other kids for not following such an important rule.

"This is a matter of safety," she says. "This is no time to be fooling around!"

Zack tries to explain that he was pushed, but the teacher will not let him speak. He wanted to tell her that it wasn't his fault.

1. If you were Zack, what would you do next?

2. Have you ever been in a situation where you needed to defend your behavior to an adult?

{ Family Discussion }

Zack is being blamed for something that he did not do. Worse, he is not being given the chance to defend himself. Sometimes when adults are wrong, it is important for you to speak up. This is not always easy. Challenging an adult who is in charge can be scary. However, if you stay calm and speak with respect, you stand a better chance of being heard. If Zack immediately starts yelling that the teacher is wrong, that will probably make the situation worse. Timing is also very important. Sometimes, waiting a while to speak is best, so you can get your thoughts together and choose your words more carefully.

Besides talking to the teacher right away, Zack could also write a letter to her when he gets home or speak to her the next day. Then again, Zack may decide it really isn't worth making a fuss. Sometimes, even when situations are unfair, we realize that they're not very important, and we let them go. But if Zack keeps thinking about what happened, he might want to talk it over with friends or with family members to see what they would do.

Breaking a New Toy

*R*yan is very excited to get a remote-control car for Christmas. He puts the batteries in and immediately starts speeding the car around the living room, crashing it into the furniture. Suddenly, the front end snaps off the car.

"I can't believe it!" Ryan exclaimed. "Mom, can you take the car back to the store and get another one? The front end just broke off!"

1. Should Ryan's mom take the car back to the store?

2. Should the store take back the car?

3. Do you think Ryan was misusing the car?

4. Do you think the car was poorly made if it couldn't hold up after being crashed into furniture?

{ *Family Discussion* }

Using something in a way that it was not intended to be used is called *misuse*. One example of misuse is using a toy car as a hammer. Some would argue that once you purchase something, you can do anything you want with it. After all, the object now belongs to you. In Ryan's case, he was using the car in a way it was not meant to be used. Since the toy now belongs to him, he can do anything he wants with it, but he must take responsibility for whatever happens.

The store has an obligation to sell goods that will last. In this case, it might be difficult to decide who is responsible for the broken toy. If the toy was broken or defective before it was purchased, the store has an obligation to offer a replacement or a refund. Some might say it is Ryan's fault for misusing the car. Then again, the car may have been poorly made and would have broken anyway, even if Ryan had used the car properly. Since Ryan misused the car, he will probably have a difficult time returning it to the store.

Taking care of the things we own is important. There are lots of things—such as a car, lawn mower, or bike—that need regular servicing in order to continue to work well. When something breaks because it was neglected or used improperly, we feel bad. That's why it's important to be responsible for the things that belong to us.

Sibling Rivalry

*J*uliet and Michael are running errands with their mom. As they browse through the department store, their mother comes across a perfect pair of tennis shoes for Michael. She asks the salesperson to bring him a pair to try on.

Juliet picks up a pair of sandals on display. "Mom, can I get these?" she asks. "No," says her mom. "I'm only buying tennis shoes today for Michael, especially since these shoes are on sale." "But that's not fair," cries Juliet. "Why does he get shoes and I don't?"

1. Do you think it's fair that only Michael gets shoes?

2. What would you do if you were their mom?

3. Have you ever been in a similar situation?

{ *Family Discussion* }

People should always be treated fairly. This does not mean that everyone has to be treated equally; it means the same rules apply to everyone. For example, it is fair for parents to request that their children help out with chores in the home. If one child is older than the other, however, the amount of work that each does may not be equal. Bedtimes are another example. While it is fair to insist that both children have bedtimes, those times may be different for each child. Some evenings one child may get more attention because she needs help with homework; other evenings the second child gets more attention because of soccer practice.

The same thing is true for Juliet and Michael. It certainly would not be right for their mom only to buy Michael shoes and never buy them for Juliet. However, their mother does not have to buy both of them shoes at the same time.

Because a parent buys something for one child and not the other does not mean that the second child is not equally loved. Sometimes it's okay not to treat everyone exactly the same way but rather to treat them as individuals and respect their differences.

Left Out

*G*loria is having a sleepover, and she has invited all the girls in her class except Melissa. "I'm not going to invite her," Gloria says to her mom. "Melissa is so mean! She doesn't get along with anyone in the class. I'm not going to have her ruin my party!"

"Imagine how you would feel being left out," asks her mother.

"But I hate her!" says Gloria. "And haven't you always told me not to be a phony? I don't want to have to pretend to like her!"

1. Are there times when it makes sense to leave someone out?

2. Can you think of a time when you were the only one left out of something? How did that make you feel?

3. If you were Gloria's mom, what would you say to Gloria, and why?

4. How could Gloria include Melissa and still have fun at her party?

{ *Family Discussion* }

Sometimes we are faced with the decision of whether or not to leave someone out. There are many times in life when we meet people whom we simply don't like, and that is okay. If we do decide to exclude them though, we should not be rude about it.

Before deciding not to invite Melissa, Gloria may want to consider how she would feel if she were not included. Sometimes there are sad things happening in someone's life that might make him or her rude, inconsiderate, or unkind—for example, an illness in the family, parents fighting, or bad grades at school. It helps if we can give people the benefit of the doubt.

If Gloria decides to invite Melissa, she may want to talk to her before the sleepover about her behavior. Perhaps Melissa could be given a job at the party, such as helping with the games. Perhaps Gloria's mom could keep an eye out for Melissa and immediately suggest a game or activity to play if Melissa starts acting up, or she could step in and tell Melissa privately that her comments are not acceptable at this party.

Teasing

*A*lex has been teasing his older sister Carly all day. Now, he's throwing pieces of paper at her. Carly finally gets so mad that she runs over to Alex and pulls his hair really hard.

"Dad!" yells Alex. "Carly pulled my hair!" He goes running into the next room to tell their father.

"Alex made me do it!" cries Carly. "He wouldn't stop teasing me!"

1. Whose fault is it that Alex's hair got pulled?

2. If you were their father, what would you say to Alex and Carly?

3. If you were Carly, what would you say to your father?

4. Have you ever gotten someone else in trouble?

{ Family Discussion }

Even though Alex is the one who had his hair pulled, he is partly responsible. By teasing his sister, Alex increased her frustration, which led to the hair pulling. Imagine if every kid in a classroom took a turn unscrewing a piece that held part of a desk together. Eventually, the desk would break and someone could get hurt. Who would be responsible? Every kid who took a turn unscrewing it—not just the unlucky last person who turned it one too many times. Though it is Carly who pulled Alex's hair, he clearly shares some of the blame. Both kids have to take responsibility for what happened.

Carly could have reacted differently to the situation. She could have called her father before she got really mad or walked away from Alex. Since she is the older sibling, she should show him the right way to behave. Although sometimes you cannot control your anger completely, you should always try to explore different ways to react when someone is bothering you, instead of pulling hair, throwing things, or doing other hurtful acts.

Cold French Fries

"*W*hat's wrong with the service at this restaurant tonight?!" gripes Mr. Jorgenson. "We've been waiting for our meal for almost 30 minutes!"

Finally the waiter arrives with the Jorgensons' food and apologizes for the delay. It seems the restaurant is one cook short in the kitchen this evening. To make matters worse, Mr. Jorgenson's fries are cold. The Jorgenson family eats the food, but they don't enjoy the meal at all.

At the end of the meal, Mr. Jorgenson herds the family out the door and into the car without paying the check. "There's no way I'm going to pay for poor service and a cold meal," he says.

1. What do you think about what Mr. Jorgenson did?

2. Is there something else he could have done?

3. Have you ever had a similar experience at a restaurant?

{ Family Discussion }

Restaurants have an obligation to their customers to provide acceptable food. In return, the customers have an obligation to pay for the food that they eat. Some might think 30 minutes is a long wait, but since the family did eat the food they were served, they have to pay for it. If Mr. Jorgenson had told the waiter the fries were cold and sent them back, then it would be acceptable not to pay for the fries.

To eat food and then not pay for it is stealing, even if the food is badly prepared. The restaurant that the Jorgenson family ate at might have had a "satisfaction guaranteed" policy, which means the restaurant will refund their money if they explain how the food or service was unacceptable. But instead of complaining to the manager about the service and food, Mr. Jorgenson got mad and stormed out.

Most restaurants want their customers to keep coming back and want to hear if people are dissatisfied with the service or food. If you are unhappy with a meal or service, it is always best to tell a manager or the owner of the company. The restaurant will find out that it needs to improve its customer service, you might get a free dessert or meal, and you won't be stealing.

Winning the Game

*I*t's the last quarter of a basketball game. According to the league rules, all the boys on the team have to play at least one quarter. In this particular game, all the boys have played two quarters except Joe and Ken, who aren't two of the team's better players. They've only played one quarter.

The team is down by four points. "Coach," ask Joe and Ken, "can we play this quarter?"

1. If you were the coach, what would you say to the boys?

2. If you were one of their teammates, how would you feel if the coach put in Joe and Ken?

3. If you were Joe or Ken, how would you feel if you didn't get to play another quarter?

4. What is more important to you: winning or giving everybody an equal chance to play?

{ *Family Discussion* }

Winning is important, but so is taking turns. If the expectation of all the boys on the team is that they will each have a turn, then Joe and Ken are being treated unfairly if the coach does not allow them to play enough. Many things in life involve taking turns, such as cars at an intersection, drinks at the water fountain, and family members doing chores around the house. If people did not take turns, there would be a lot more arguing in the world.

The coach should give Joe and Ken a second turn to play, even though it means that the team might lose the game. One of the reasons people play on teams is so all the players can support each other and feel like they belong. Even if some players are worse than others, they are still members of the team. How can a weaker player get more experience if he is not given enough chances to play? The better players on the team also need to understand that while winning is important, working together as a team is important, too. By letting each player have a more equal amount of playing time, everyone learns something about teamwork.

Returning a TV

*B*ill and his wife are taking their children on a camping vacation in the family van. Since their boys have a lot of energy, Bill decides to buy a small television unit with a built-in VCR that can operate off the van's cigarette lighter. This will keep the boys occupied during the long drive and any rainy days. The store manager assures Bill that if he is not satisfied, he can return the unit after one week for a full refund.

Bill is careful to save the box and receipt. He loads the mini-unit into the van and off they go. The weather is wonderful and the boys are kept so busy that they only use the TV a few times. At the end of the week, Bill repackages the TV into the box and returns it to the store for a full refund.

1. What do you think about what Bill did?

2. Should the store take back the TV?

3. Do you think this is stealing?

4. Does it matter how many times the family watched TV?

This is tricky because no one seems hurt by this. The store clerk does not feel bad if Bill returns the television and what Bill did was entirely legal. The store's policy says it's okay to return items. But this case seems to be a form of stealing.

Bill and his family have used the merchandise but have not paid for it. Some people buy dresses, wear them to a party, and then return them the next day. Other people eat half of a meal at a restaurant and then claim it was no good and refuse to pay for it.

There are many things in the world that are legally okay to do but are still wrong. For instance, if you witness someone shoplifting and do not say anything about it, you cannot be legally punished, but it is still wrong not to speak up. Or if you pass the scene of an auto accident and do not stop to help, it is legally okay but morally wrong.

Sometimes doing the right thing means going beyond the letter of the law—going out of our way to act morally. Bill could set a good example for his kids by keeping the merchandise they used.

Accepting an Apology

*S*chool has just let out, and Sue is very upset. She had confided in Haley about her feelings for José, trusting Haley not to repeat a word of it. Now she has learned that Haley told several other girls! "I trusted you with my secret," she says to Haley. "When I told you about José, you promised never to tell anyone. I am so embarrassed. You humiliated me in front of everyone! I am never talking to you again as long as I live! "

Haley feels horrible about what she did. She didn't mean to hurt Sue's feelings. "Sue, please listen to me. I realize it was very wrong of me to tell the other girls that you liked José. I feel really bad about breaking your trust. I am really sorry," Haley says.

1. Should Sue accept Haley's apology?

2. If you were Haley, how would you have apologized?

3. If you were Haley, what would you do now?

4. Can you think of a time when someone didn't accept your apology?

{ *Family Discussion* }

Not only should we apologize to someone when we do something wrong, but we also should try to accept others' apologies when they wrong us. Not to accept an apology is to remain mad. It means we keep the hurt feelings alive and harbor bad feelings against the person who wronged us. When we accept an apology, it doesn't mean that we have to forget what the other person did to us. Accepting an apology simply means that we are ready to move on and begin to let that wound heal.

When best friends like Haley and Sue have a fight, just allowing the other person the opportunity to apologize is important. Since these two girls will probably stay in the same classes, it will be easier for them to see each other if they resolve this problem by giving—and accepting—an apology.

Caught Between Two Parents

*L*ife has been pretty tough for Meiko since her parents separated. Now, Thanksgiving is approaching. It is Sunday afternoon, and Meiko's mom is arguing on the phone with Meiko's dad about their plans for the Thanksgiving holiday. Her mom says that she is planning to take Meiko out of town for Thanksgiving, so she can see her grandparents. Her dad wants Meiko to spend Thanksgiving with him, especially since Meiko was with her mom for two weeks during summer vacation and also had her eleventh birthday party with her.

"I'm not going to argue about it," her mom says. "Let's let Meiko decide. She is certainly old enough to make this kind of decision. "

1. Should Meiko have to choose, or should her parents choose for her?

2. If you were Meiko, what would you do?

3. How else do you think Meiko's parents could make this decision?

4. Have you ever had to choose between two parents, siblings, or friends?

{ Family Discussion }

It is unfair to put a child between two fighting parents. It is also unfair to ask a child to have to choose between parents. Even though Meiko's parents are not living with one another anymore, they are still Meiko's parents. As her parents, it is their responsibility to make the decision. Though it may be difficult for them, it would be even more difficult for Meiko. They will need to figure out between themselves how to solve this dilemma.

Her parents could agree that Meiko will spend alternate Thanksgivings with each of them. They could ask another adult, such as a family therapist, religious leader, or school guidance counselor, to help them make the decision. They could even flip a coin! Any of these ways of choosing is better than making Meiko decide between her mom and her dad. It is okay for them to consult Meiko, but the final decision should be made by her parents.

Too High a Profit?

*O*ne very hot Sunday afternoon, Jenny and Carly decide to buy lemons, cups, and ice. They set up a card table and sell lemonade in front of their home to make some extra money.

Jenny wants to sell each cup for a dollar, but Carly isn't sure about the price. The lemonade only cost them 10 cents a cup to make, and Carly doesn't think they should charge their customers so much money for each cup.

1. Is it fair to charge so much money for a cup of lemonade?

2. How much would you charge? Why?

3. Do you think it would make a difference if the money they made was going to a charity?

4. If you were Jenny, what would you say to Carly to convince her that a dollar is a fair amount?

{ Family Discussion }

It is common and acceptable to sell an item for more than we originally paid. Making a profit is part of business. No one forces customers to buy a product. If a price is set too high for a product or service, the customers can simply decide not to buy it or to look elsewhere for a less-expensive price.

It does, however, matter how we make a profit. For example, it is not right for the power companies to sell electricity, which everyone needs, for a very high profit. And it is not right to lie about a product in order to make a profit. If we hire employees to help us make a product, it is not right to underpay them or have them work in unsafe conditions. Having a business and making money is fine, but we should do it safely and honestly.

Jenny and Carly are not doing anything misleading or dishonest, but they may find they have to lower the cost of their lemonade in order to sell it. Carly is probably right that they are charging too much for a glass of lemonade, but there is nothing morally wrong about it.

The Snow Shovelers

George wants to make a little money and decides to start a business. He is going to knock on his neighbors' doors and see if they will hire him to shovel the snow off their front walks.

He hangs a sign around his neck that reads, "Snow Shoveling $5.00" and walks up and down the block. Mark, who lives three houses away, sees George with the sign, and thinks it's a pretty good idea. A few minutes later, Mark comes outside and starts to knock on the neighbors' doors. He is wearing a sign that reads, "Snow Shoveling $4.00."

1. What do you think about what Mark did?

2. Does it make a difference if George thought up the idea first?

3. Is it fair for Mark to charge less than George?

4. What should George do?

{ Family Discussion }

There is nothing wrong with competition in business. For customers, competition may mean lower prices or better service. Imagine if there was just one company that sold fast-food hamburgers! It is not fair to compete by lying about your product or service or telling lies about the competition, but a little competition is usually better for everyone.

Even though competition is a part of life, it is not fair to steal someone else's idea. Varying the idea a little is better than doing exactly the same thing the competition is doing. George needs to talk to Mark about this. There are several ways they could be friendly competitors. For instance, they could decide to each cover a different part of the neighborhood. They could even go into business together, share their profits, and sell their services for the same amount.

Giving Money to Someone in Need

Juanita and her mom are leaving the toy store after finishing their holiday shopping. They pass by a man sitting on the ground playing the guitar. Next to the man is a cup with some coins in it.

Juanita has some money in her pocket that she got for her allowance. "Mom," she asks, "can I put a quarter in his cup?"

1. What would you say if you were Juanita's mom?

2. Would you put money in the man's cup or not?

3. How can you tell if a person really needs the money he is asking for?

4. Can you think of some ways in which your family helps others out?

{ *Family Discussion* }

Some people are poor because they lose their job and cannot find another one. Sometimes people are too sick to work or don't have the skills needed to get a job: for instance, they don't know the language, they can't read, or they don't have enough education. Many of these people are homeless because without a job, they can't afford to pay rent.

One of our purposes in life is to bring more goodness into the world—to make it a better place for ourselves and for others. We can do this by giving money to needy people on the street or by donating money, goods, or services to a charity. We can purchase extra food at the store and donate it to a food bank, or we can donate old clothes and blankets to a shelter for homeless people.

Some people don't give money to strangers because they believe the person on the street might be "faking it" or isn't interested in working. Others may think that the person is begging for money to buy alcohol or drugs. Many people on the streets who are begging, however, are embarrassed to beg. It is very hard to stand or sit, day after day, and ask people for money. Most people who are asking for money really need it. Since we can't tell who does or doesn't really need it, it is better for us to assume that they are being truthful, so that we may help them.

Teamwork

*I*t is the tenth softball game of the season, and the team is behind by two runs. The team is at bat when suddenly the coach is distracted by two of his players, Collin and Mitch, wrestling in the dugout. After separating the two of them, he learns that Collin was taunting Mitch, saying that he threw the ball like a three-year-old. Then Mitch told Collin that he couldn't hit a ball if he tried.

The coach has been lecturing the boys about teamwork. Now he's faced with pulling Mitch and Collin out of the game as a lesson to them and the other boys on the team. If he does this, there is a good chance the team will lose this game. If he doesn't, what sort of example will that be?

1. If you were the coach, what would you do?

2. Do you think teamwork or winning is more important?

3. What other options does the coach have?

4. Would pulling Mitch and Collin out of the game be fair to the other boys, if it means that they'll lose the game?

{ *Family Discussion* }

Teamwork is very important in life. There are certain things that we can't do alone. Firefighters at a fire, sailors on a boat, police responding to a bank robbery, and construction workers building a home are all examples of people working together. In a team, everyone has a job. Winning and being successful are important, but so is working together with others.

Team members have a responsibility to their teammates to play their best, but they also have a responsibility to make sure everyone else on the team gets along. Teammates should encourage and support each other.

Instead of jeopardizing the game, the coach could call a time out and give the boys a chance to apologize to one another. Or he might figure out a way to bench one player from part of the game and the other player from another part of the game. Mitch and Collin need to learn that making fun of a teammate because of a bad play or a losing game, is to miss what sports is all about—working together.

When a Friend Needs Help

School starts at 8:15 a.m. Ariel's third-grade teacher is very serious about his students arriving on time, and Ariel has never been late to class. She makes it a point to be sitting in her seat at 8:10 a.m. every morning.

This morning, though, as she is walking to school, she notices that her friend, Li, is frantically gathering her belongings from the sidewalk. "My backpack wasn't zipped and all my stuff fell out," Li says.

Ariel looks at her watch. She has about seven minutes to get to class. She'll never make it on time if she helps Li. She looks down at Li kneeling on the ground, gathering pencils and pens from the concrete.

1. If you were Ariel, would you stop and help Li?

2. If you were Li, how would you feel if Ariel stopped to help? What about if Ariel hurried to get to class and didn't help?

3. Have you ever been late to an event because you stopped to help someone?

4. If you were Ariel's teacher, what would be your response if she came in late and told this story?

{ *Family Discussion* }

Being on time is important, especially when there are rules about it, like in Ariel's class. But sometimes things come up and we have to be late for appointments, classes, or even dinner. When we are not on time for something, we should always consider the people who might be waiting for us, or things that can't begin without us. If we can, it is best to let people know that we will be late.

In this situation, Ariel needs to decide what is more important to her—helping a friend or not being tardy to class. She needs to figure out her *priorities*. Often we must decide between the importance of one thing over another. Although Ariel's teacher disapproves of students arriving late to his class, he will likely understand her being late this time, once she explains the circumstances. Sometimes it's okay to change your routine—like Ariel's outstanding record of being early every day—if something more important comes up. Good friends often help each other out even when it inconveniences them or disrupts their normal routine.

Siblings to the Rescue

Shelly and Tracy are sisters. They go to school together, but are two grades apart. Sometimes they see each other at lunchtime, but Shelly doesn't pay much attention to Tracy. After all, Tracy is younger and hangs out with the "babies."

One day at lunch, Shelly and her friends are sitting a few benches away from Tracy. Shelly notices that some kids are picking on Tracy. They are taking her drink and giving her a hard time. Shelly is afraid that her friends will roll their eyes if they see her helping her younger sister, but she doesn't like people treating Tracy that way.

1. What would you do if you were Shelly?

2. As a friend of Shelly's, how would you react if she helped out Tracy?

3. Are brothers and sisters obligated to help each other out?

{ Family Discussion }

Some siblings are embarrassed to be seen with a younger sister or brother in public. Sometimes it is easier to speak up if a friend is being teased than it is to defend a member of our family.

Sibling relationships are special and are different than relationships with our friends. Two people who are related will be related forever. No matter how difficult life may be, we should always be able to feel safe with members of our family and to count on them to help us when we are in need. Family members have an obligation to help each other feel safe, both inside and outside the home. Even when you might not be getting along with your brother or sister, it is more important to help him or her than to worry about feeling embarrassed in front of your friends.

Trouble in the Classroom

Mr. Ramirez is very upset with his class. Not only have a number of the students failed to do their homework assignments, but now several of them are being disruptive.

"I've about had it with this class today," he says. "The next disruption is going to cost all of you recess time." A few minutes later, Mr. Ramirez sees a student flick a wad of paper across the room.

"That's it!" says Mr. Ramirez. "No recess for the entire class today!"

1. Is it fair that everyone is to be punished?

2. Is there another way Mr. Ramirez might have dealt with this?

3. Have you ever been in a similar situation?

{ Family Discussion }

Whenever we are a part of a larger group, we are affected by the actions of everyone in the group. This is true for everyone—people who work together, members of families, and students in classes. Sometimes it may not seem fair to be punished or held responsible for another's actions, but it is a fact of life that this happens.

One person's decision or action often affects a larger group of people. For instance, people lose their jobs when a company goes out of business, even though it may only be because one person made a bad decision. If one team member fumbles the ball, the whole team may lose the game. If someone spills a drink on the ice, the rink may have to be shut down while the mess is cleaned. There is a well-known story of two men fishing in a rowboat on a lake. Suddenly, one of the men begins drilling a hole in the bottom of the boat.

"What are you doing?!" cries his companion.

"Don't worry," the first man says. "I'm only drilling the hole under *my* seat."

We should always remember that it is our duty to act responsibly—other people may be affected by our actions.

Too Many Worthy Causes

*N*oah's mom comes home from work one day. She opens the mail after greeting her son.

"Look at all these solicitation letters that came today in the mail," she says to Noah. "Here's one to help save the gray wolf, another to send medicine to children overseas, and a third to build a new library in town. I'd like to donate to a charity, but it is hard to choose which one to give to."

1. Should Noah and his mom give a little to each of the three charities or just give to one?

2. If you were Noah, which one would you choose?

3. Do you think it is important to help people in your community first, or is it sometimes better to help people in another country?

4. Does your family give to a charity? If your family does give, why does it choose to give to that particular charity?

{ Family Discussion }

It seems that almost every day another letter arrives in the mail asking for a contribution to a worthy cause. Sometimes it is difficult to decide which ones to support. Some people decide based on the urgency of the situation. People who are hungry or terminally ill are in greater immediate need than a political campaign or library fund-raising effort. Many people feel they should help human beings who are in trouble before animals who are in distress. Some people want their donations to go toward improving the community in which they live, while others think it is more important to help people of their own religion. Still others give only to one or two causes they feel very strongly about. Whichever organizations you choose to support, you should consider your decision carefully.

Changing Your Mind

*T*wo weeks ago, Laurie was invited to Christina's swim party. Laurie's mom called up Christina's mom and said that Laurie would love to go.

One hour before the party, Laurie tells her mom that she is very tired, doesn't feel like swimming, and wants to stay home. She asks her mom to call and say that she will not be coming to the party. Laurie's mom knows that Christina will be very disappointed if Laurie doesn't come, especially since Christina was limited to five friends for her party. Perhaps if she had known Laurie wasn't coming, she would have invited another friend to take her place.

1. If you were Laurie's mom, what would you do?

2. How would you feel if you were Christina?

3. Have you ever changed your mind about going somewhere?

4. Do you think an hour before the party is enough notice to cancel?

{ *Family Discussion* }

When we give our word, we want people to know that they can count on us. However, there will occasionally be times when we need to cancel plans we've made. For example, we cannot go to a party when we are sick, even though we had planned on going. When considering a change of plans, we need to think about how the change will affect other people. In this situation, Christina will be disappointed that Laurie won't be coming.

It would not be right for Laurie's mom to force her to go to the party. There are, however, compromises that can be considered. Laurie could go to the party but not go swimming. She could go to the party but only stay for a short time. Or she could offer to take Christina out for an ice cream cone the following day and give Christina her gift. In any case, whatever Laurie decides to do, she needs to call Christina to apologize for not coming to the party.

Pet Chores

*M*alcolm really wanted a dog! For months he had asked his father for one. His dad, however, wasn't so sure, because taking care of a dog is a lot of work. Finally Malcolm's dad made a deal with him. If Malcolm would feed the dog in the morning and evening and take him for a walk each day when he came home from school, then his dad would let him have a dog. Malcolm agreed to his dad's terms, and he got a dog named Sparky.

Malcolm loves Sparky, and his dad loves him, too. But after feeding Sparky for three weeks, there were several times when Malcolm forgot to feed him. He also had to be reminded to walk him after school. Malcolm tells his dad that with all his homework and sports, he just doesn't have the time to take care of the dog.

"Well, I'm sorry Malcolm," says his dad. "But I'm going to have to take Sparky back to the pound."

"But this is Sparky's home," says Malcolm. "I love him and he loves me!"

1. If you were Malcolm's dad, what would you say to Malcolm?

2. If you were Malcolm, what would you do?

3. Should Malcolm be given a second chance?

{ *Family Discussion* }

It is important to follow through with the promises we make. To make a commitment and follow through is the mature and responsible thing to do. Some promises are more important than others, especially if not keeping them will affect others. However, sometimes in spite of our good intentions, the commitment is greater than we anticipate.

Malcolm loves his dog and wants to keep him. To accomplish this, he will need some help changing his daily routine to include caring for Sparky. It takes time and several reminders before a new chore becomes a part of our daily life. To help him remember, Malcolm could put a sign on the refrigerator that says, "Please feed me. Love, Sparky." On the other hand, it may not have been fair for Malcolm's dad to expect Malcolm to take care of the dog all by himself. Malcolm and his dad need to talk about the situation and work out a new deal so they can keep Sparky, such as sharing the responsibilities of walking him.

Different Families, Different Rules

*J*eannie, twelve years old, is spending the night at her friend Kerry's house; Kerry's parents are taking the girls out for dinner and a movie. At dinner, Kerry's parents decide they will go see the new action thriller. This sounds great to Kerry and Jeannie, especially since everyone at school has been talking about this new movie.

When they get to the theater, Jeannie reads the billboard and discovers that the movie is rated "R." Her parents do not allow her to see R-rated movies.

1. If you were Jeannie, what would you do?

2. Is it okay for Jeannie to see the movie because she's with Kerry's parents?

3. At what age, do you think, is it okay to see R- or NC-17-rated movies?

4. Can you think of a rule in your family that is different in a friend's family?

{ *Family Discussion* }

This is a difficult situation for Jeannie. It's hard for her to say no to Kerry's parents, especially since she's their guest. As a guest, Jeannie feels she is supposed to go along with her hosts' decision. If her parents trust Kerry's parents enough to let her sleep over, perhaps seeing the movie is all right.

This is a situation where two families have different values—not necessarily better or worse, but different. Other examples of different values might include bedtime hours, going-out policies, curfews, homework rules, etc.

While it is usually good manners to go along with what your host is doing, there are times when we may need to speak up, especially if it is an activity that bothers us or we know is not appropriate in our family. Speaking up, especially when the decision involves adults, is often hard to do. Jeannie might explain the problem to her friend and ask her to speak to her parents. Jeannie might also ask Kerry's parents if she could phone home to see if it's okay with her folks for her to see the movie.

Gossiping

Max is having lunch with a bunch of friends from school. They start talking about how weird their friend Taylor has become. She's always walking with her head down, she doesn't smile anymore, and she never wants to hang out with her friends.

Max is upset by his friends' gossip. He can't stand to hear the other kids talking about Taylor this way. Taylor has confided in Max that her father is very sick and that her family might have to sell their house and move away. Max knows that the other kids don't know the whole story, but he doesn't want to tell them everything. He has promised he will keep Taylor's secret.

1. If you were Max, what would you say?

2. Is there a way for Max to defend Taylor, without breaking her confidence?

3. What do you think about her friends talking about Taylor behind her back?

{ *Family Discussion* }

Max has been entrusted with a secret, and it is his obligation to keep that information private. Max could correct the others by telling them *some* of the truth. He could say he has heard Taylor has problems at home. That could, however, lead to speculation among their friends.

Whether the statements are true or false, talking about someone else when they are not there is gossip. Gossip hurts people's feelings. Too often, a nice comment about someone is followed by a cutting comment. "Doesn't Vera have beautiful hair?" is frequently followed by something like, "Yeah, but she dresses so weird."

Max can keep silent and let the others put down Taylor, share her secret and betray her trust, or he can excuse himself from the conversation. Sometimes walking away from gossip is the best way to avoid it. As a last resort, Max can explain to his friends that Taylor is upset about something—without giving away her secret.

The Deal

$\mathcal{T}$om is selling his old bike. Mike comes along, looks it over carefully, and offers to buy it for $15. Even though Tom was hoping for $20, he accepts Mike's offer.

Mike promises to return within the hour and goes home to get the money. A few minutes after Mike leaves, Charlie comes by, sees the bike, pulls out his wallet, and tells Tom that he'll buy it for $20.

1. What should Tom do?

2. Would it be different if Charlie also offered $15 but had the money with him?

3. If Tom does decide to sell Charlie the bike, what will he tell Mike when Mike returns?

4. What could Tom do differently the next time?

{ Family Discussion }

There is no higher degree of trust than when you give your word to someone else and that person accepts it. In this case, a promise is a promise. Mike has agreed to buy the bike, and Tom has agreed to sell it to him. It would not be fair for either one to go back on his word. Since the boys agreed that Mike would come back in an hour with the money, Tom needs to wait for an hour before he can accept another offer. If an hour passes and Mike does not come back, then his agreement with Tom is no longer binding, and Tom is free to sell the bike to Charlie.

Part of being a business person is maintaining your honesty and integrity. Tom can learn from this situation and consider asking a little more for what he is selling next time, but to go back on his word now would be breaking a promise.

A Better Offer

*F*our weeks ago, Sara agreed to baby-sit for the Bergers on Saturday night so they could go to a family wedding. But on Thursday afternoon, Sara was invited to a ski weekend with her best friend and her family. Sara loves skiing and doesn't get the opportunity to go very often.

Sara calls one of her friends who agrees to fill in for her Saturday night. Sara then calls Mrs. Berger to explain the situation. She offers to come by the Bergers on Friday with her friend so they can meet her.

"I'm sorry, Sara," says Mrs. Berger, "but you promised me that you would come and baby-sit. This won't work for me. I just don't feel comfortable leaving the kids with someone they don't know."

1. If you were Sara, what would you do?

2. Is it fair of Mrs. Berger to reject Sara's solution?

3. What else could Sara do?

4. What else might Mrs. Berger do?

{ Family Discussion }

A *compromise* is when people agree to give in a little, so together they can reach a reasonable solution to a problem. In a compromise, no one person gets *everything* he or she wants, but each gets at least a little.

It is necessary, in life, to compromise with others. Moms and dads continually compromise. Divorced couples make compromises when it comes to raising their children. Good friends make compromises concerning how they will spend their time together. Brothers and sisters have to compromise, and so do people at work. People who can't ever compromise are often thought of as selfish, because they always want everything their way.

Mrs. Berger could compromise by agreeing to meet Sara's friend to see if she might be a good sitter. Sara has already offered part of a compromise by finding a replacement and bringing her over to the Bergers' home. Sara could also offer to baby-sit along with her friend for a couple of hours on Friday so her friend and the children can get to know each other a little. If Mrs. Berger does compromise, she may find that instead of just one good baby-sitter, she'll have two.

A Dangerous Secret

*R*oberta adores her older sister, Julie. One afternoon, Julie confides her plans for the evening to Roberta: she needs Roberta's help to sneak out of the house to visit her girlfriend. She tells Roberta that if their mom asks where she is, Roberta should say that Julie went to bed. Julie reminds her how important it is to keep the secret, and Roberta swears she won't tell.

Later that afternoon, Roberta overhears Julie on the phone with her girlfriend talking about their evening activities. Julie plans to sneak some alcohol from the liquor cabinet when she leaves. Then she and her girlfriend will drive in her friend's car to a party across town.

1. If you were Roberta, what would you do?

2. Is Julie expecting too much from Roberta by asking her to keep the secret?

3. If Roberta keeps the secret, do you think she should get in trouble if Julie gets caught?

4. Can you think of some secrets it might not be right to keep?

{ *Family Discussion* }

If someone trusts you with a secret, it is your duty not to tell it to anyone. But if keeping a secret for someone puts that person in danger, you have a responsibility to tell others to prevent that person or others from getting hurt. If a friend tells you that she is going to hurt herself, or if you hear of a crime that is going to be committed, you have an obligation to tell the secret. If Roberta thinks her sister is going to be driving and drinking, she needs to tell Julie that she won't keep her secret.

Roberta could also tell Julie that she thinks her plan is dangerous. She can threaten to tell their mom, or she can simply tell Julie that she won't lie for her. Roberta could also decide to tell their mom that she thinks Julie is going to sneak out.

Julie has put her sister in an uncomfortable situation. There is a big difference between asking someone to keep a secret and asking him or her to lie. It is very important to remember that secrets involving danger should never stay secret. Julie is probably going to be furious with Roberta for telling, but protecting someone from possible harm is more important than that person's hurt or angry feelings.

"Are You a Chicken?"

Jim moved into the neighborhood recently and doesn't have any friends. All the guys on the block seem to hang around with one another, and he desperately wants to join them. He has become a little friendly with one of the boys, Peter.

Today, while Jim is sitting on his front steps, Peter comes by with a few boys and invites Jim to come with them. They go around the corner and each of the boys picks up a rock and tries to hit a neighbor's dog tied up in the backyard.

Jim picks up a stone, but hesitates. "Come on," one of the boys calls to him. "What are you, a chicken?"

1. If you were Jim, what would you say?

2. What do you think about what Peter and his friends are doing to the dog?

3. If Jim decides not to join in, does he also have an obligation to tell the boys not to throw the rocks?

4. Can you think of a time when you were faced with having to say no?

{ *Family Discussion* }

Saying "no" is difficult. It may mean losing friends, and it may mean that others make fun of us. It takes a lot of courage to say "no" when everyone around us is saying "yes." No matter how old we are, there will always be times like this. You may have heard a saying, *If everyone were jumping off a cliff, would you follow them?* It is important for us to think for ourselves and to make our own decisions.

This is a tough decision for Jim. He really wants to make friends with the other boys, but he doesn't want to hurt the dog. It will take real courage for him to say no. Maybe there is something else he could do, such as make an excuse that his throwing arm is healing from an injury, or throw the rock but deliberately miss. Jim may also think about whether he wants to try to stop the other boys from throwing the rocks by yelling at them, threatening to tell the neighbor, or getting help from an adult. Saying no may cost him their friendship. If Jim chooses to throw the rock and continues to develop a friendship with these boys, he is likely to find himself in other difficult situations. Jim would be better off finding a group of friends whose values are closer to his own.

The Eyewitness

*I*t's Monday after school, and Jamal is walking home with a few friends. They take a shortcut through the park and see two older boys spray-painting swear words on a wall near the swings.

The next day at school, a special assembly is called. "I am sorry to inform you," says the principal, "that yesterday afternoon, vandals spray-painted all over the children's playground next to the school. If any of you knows anything about this, I expect to hear from you by the end of the day. Even if you weren't the ones who did it, if you don't come forward, you will be just as guilty as those who did participate."

After the assembly, one of the older boys walks up to Jamal in the hall. "Listen, you creep," the boy says to Jamal, "if you or your friends say one word about seeing us in the park yesterday, we're going to make you sorry!"

1. If you were Jamal, what would you do?

2. If you were Jamal, what would you do if you wanted to tell but the others didn't?

3. Is the principal being fair?

4. When is it okay to tell on someone else?

{ Family Discussion }

If Jamal doesn't tell what he saw, he will be helping the boys get away with their wrongdoing. In American law, this is called being *an accessory to a crime.* The getaway driver in a bank robbery is just as guilty of breaking the law as the robbers with the guns. There are probably many times that you've seen people doing something wrong—littering, stealing, or picking on someone—and didn't do anything about it. If people do something wrong the first time and "get away with it," they are more likely to do it again.

If Jamal does tell who did the spray-painting, he might get in trouble with the older boys. Maybe Jamal can tell the principal that he knows older kids did the spray-painting but refuse to reveal their names to protect himself and his friends. The principal should accept this and work on finding ways to keep the school grounds safe in the future. It might be a good idea for Jamal to talk with his parents, a relative, or a teacher about his dilemma. Sometimes it helps to get another perspective when you have a problem.

An Intolerant Friend

*a*nna is friends with Carla, even though many of the other girls in school think Carla is rude. However, Anna was disturbed when Carla refused to take an open spot at the lunch table and said, "I'm not going to sit next to those Mexicans!" Last week, when Carla said something about one of their classmates and Anna told her that it wasn't nice, Carla looked at her like she was weird. Anna's been over to Carla's house and knows that her father is intolerant, too.

Now Carla has just made another racial slur, and Anna can't stand to hear her talk this way.

1. If you were Anna, what would you say to Carla?

2. Would you continue to be friends with Carla?

3. Is it Carla's fault that she's so rude?

4. What's so bad about racial insults, anyway?

{ *Family Discussion* }

Racism is when we treat people of different races unfairly or badly because of the color of their skin or their physical appearance. People who are racist believe everyone in a racial group behaves and thinks the same way. Rather than getting to know someone as a person, with a unique personality and individual strengths and weaknesses, racists assume all people of the same race are identical. Racists also believe their racial group is better or "superior" to other racial groups.

Anna can decide to stop being friends with Carla, keep silent, or speak honestly to Carla about her racism. Anna could say, "Carla, it makes me really uncomfortable when you say things like that. Please don't do it anymore. If you keep saying these kinds of awful things, I'm not going to hang around with you."

Cheating

*I*t's third period, and the algebra test is just moments away. As Rosa and Judy settle into their seats, Judy turns to Rosa and whispers that she didn't have time to study for the test because she was up all night practicing her lines for the play audition. She asks Rosa if she can copy answers from her paper.

Rosa knows that it is wrong to let Judy copy, but Judy is Rosa's best friend, and she really wants Judy to get the part in the play.

1. If you were Rosa, what would you do?

2. If Judy did not have time to study, what other options did she have besides copying from Rosa's paper?

3. Is there a kind way that Rosa can say no to Judy?

4. Have you ever been unprepared for a test? How did that feel?

{ *Family Discussion* }

Whether it is a little cheating or major cheating, what Judy wants to do is not honest. Taking someone else's work and presenting it as our own is a form of stealing. Copying sentences from a book and presenting them as ours, which is called *plagiarism*, is dishonest and also illegal.

In the business world, companies and individuals protect the work that they have done by obtaining a trademark, patent, or copyright. This means that they are the only people who can use their logo, slogan, product, or character. Inventors patent their inventions so people can't copy their ideas. When you think of or create something unique, you want to be able to take credit for your work.

To allow someone to copy from your paper is to go along with the stealing, and this is wrong. Rosa could say, "I'm sorry that you didn't have time to prepare for the test, but I can't let you copy my answers. Maybe you can talk to the teacher and see if he'll let you take a make-up test tomorrow."

Just One Smoke

*O*n the weekends, Carter hangs out with a bunch of boys who usually meet at the park to play ball. This Sunday, Al has an idea. "Hey, you guys, I took these cigarettes from my father. Let's smoke them."

Carter has never tried cigarettes before, and he is kind of curious. He would never start smoking or become addicted, but why not at least try it?

As the boys head around the corner, Al asks, "Hey, Carter, you coming with us?"

1. If you were Carter, what would you do?

2. If you were Al, what would you say to Carter if he says no?

3. Is there harm in experimenting?

4. Can you think of something that is not good for you but that you feel would be okay to try in a small amount?

{ Family Discussion }

Even though Carter is not being pressured directly to try smoking, all of his friends are clearly going to smoke. Carter will feel pressured by his friends' actions. The ways we respond to pressures to belong—such as wearing the right clothes, using certain language, and coloring our hair—are all ways of finding out who we are and what we like.

We all have to try new things at one time or another. When we do try some new things for the first time, we need to be careful and not overdo it. Moderation should be the key in all of our habits. Too much of anything is not good for us, whether it is sun, exercise, or even dessert!

But some experimentation is dangerous no matter how old we are, or how moderately we do it. For instance, moderate drinking and then driving is not acceptable. In this case, Carter only wants to try smoking one cigarette. One cigarette may seem harmless, but even one is bad for you and could possibly lead to smoking another one. It's up to Carter to decide what is more important: his fear of possibly being put down by his friends or doing what he knows is right.

Telltale Signs

Sarah's mom is one of several parents involved in a carpool. For the past two Monday afternoons when she's picked up the other ninth-graders from school, she has noticed that Diana's eyes are red and there is the smell of marijuana smoke on her clothes. Sarah's mom considers whether she should speak to Diana or call her mother. She decides to talk to her ninth-grade daughter first.

"Mom," her daughter tells her, "it's none of your business! If you tell Diana's mom, she's going to get into big trouble. What do you think she's going to think of me if you tell on her?"

1. If you were Sarah's mom, what would you do?

2. If you were Sarah, what could you do?

3. Is this Sarah's mom's business?

4. If you were Diana, would you rather have Sarah's mom talk to you or to your mom ?

{ Family Discussion }

Even though Diana is not her daughter, Sarah's mom feels she has a responsibility to Diana because she cares about her. When a foul ball flies into the stands, we shout, "Heads up!" If we see someone driving at night without their lights on, we signal to remind them to turn their headlights on. We do these things because we don't want anyone to get hurt.

If Sarah doesn't think her mom should get involved, perhaps there is something she could do, such as talk to Diana and tell her that her mom is concerned that Diana is doing drugs. Sarah might also say that she, too, is concerned for Diana's health and has been wondering if she would like to talk to Sarah about her situation. Sarah's mom will have to decide how she should handle the situation in a way that will best help Diana. If Sarah's mom decides she is going to tell Diana's mom, she should tell Diana first.

Raising a Grade

*S*teve is the star quarterback on his school's football team. The school's policy states that, in order to play sports, athletes must maintain at least a 3.0 grade-point average. Steve has just received his midterm grades and they are just below 3.0. His spot on the team is in jeopardy unless he can get one grade changed. He decides to speak to his English teacher about possibly changing his C to a B–.

Even though it is against school policy for teachers to change grades, Steve is sure Mr. Leder will understand. After all, Mr. Leder is a graduate of the school and once played on the football team himself. Steve goes to see Mr. Leder and pleads with him to raise his grade so he can remain on the team.

1. If you were Mr. Leder, what would you do?

2. What else could Steve do?

3. Do you think Steve should be treated differently because he's on the football team? Would you feel the same way if he was in the school play?

{ Family Discussion }

It's not fair to have one standard for all the other kids in class and another one for the school athletes. When two people are treated differently in the same situation, it's called a *double standard.*

Sometimes there are good and fair reasons for treating two people differently. If a basketball team is choosing players, one boy might get chosen to play center because he is taller. But there are also times when two people who are relatively the same are treated differently. This is not fair.

Instead of asking for special treatment, Steve should allow himself to be put on probation from the team for the next marking period. This way he can study harder to raise his grade-point average and then play next season.

The Hungry Shopper

*I*t is lunchtime, and Robbie and his mom are in the supermarket.

"Mommy, I'm hungry!" says Robbie. His mom wheels the cart around to the fruit section and gives him a small cluster of organic grapes to eat.

"There," she says. "That should hold you until we get home for lunch."

1. Was it okay for Robbie's mom to give him the grapes?

2. Would it make a difference if the fruit was slightly bruised anyway, so it was clear that no one was going to buy it?

3. Do you think Robbie's mom should tell the cashier at the checkout stand about the grapes? Would that make eating the grapes before paying for them okay?

{ *Family Discussion* }

Taking something that is not yours is wrong, whether it is a small toy, a pack of gum, a flower

from a neighbor's garden, or a few grapes from the market. Even if you intend to pay for the item

later, you must first ask permission. To take something, no matter how little, and not pay for it,

is stealing. If everyone took a cluster of grapes without paying for them, the store would lose a

lot of money.

Finders, Keepers

$\mathcal{T}$he bell just rang to signal the end of lunch, and Raphael is the last kid to gather his things before returning to class. As he hurries to throw away his trash, he notices a pack of baseball cards under a bench. Raphael's hobby is collecting baseball cards. The cards he has found are pretty rare—and they are cards he doesn't own.

"Wow, it would be great to add these cards to my collection!" Raphael thinks.

1. What would you do if you were Raphael?

2. Since Raphael found the cards, do they belong to him?

3. If Raphael had found a radio or a watch, would the situation be different?

4. Have you ever found something valuable? What did you do with it?

{ Family Discussion }

It is likely that baseball cards found under a bench were dropped accidentally by their owner, although it is possible that someone left the cards as trash. Raphael should try to locate the owner or turn the cards into the school's lost-and-found office, and let the school officials take responsibility for them. If Raphael decides to try to find the owner, he should announce that he found some baseball cards. If the owner can identify which ones they are or where they were lost, Raphael will have to return them.

Lost property is property that belongs to someone else, not to us. If property was not obviously left there on purpose, like things put out by the curb to be thrown out or something found in the trash, we should assume that its owner accidentally misplaced it. Sometimes people offer rewards for returning lost property. But the best reason to return something is not for the reward, but because it's the right thing to do.

Littering

as Kim and Valerie are walking home from school, Kim drops the core of an apple she has been eating into a bush.

"Hey, don't do that!" Valerie says.

"What's the big deal?" Kim replies. "It's not like I littered or anything. It'll disintegrate in time, anyway. In fact, it's probably good for the plants."

1. What do you think about Kim dropping the apple core?

2. Would it make a difference if it were a candy wrapper?

3. What would you have done if you were Valerie?

4. Have you ever littered?

{ *Family Discussion* }

Yes, it is true that an apple core will disintegrate and will do so far faster than a candy wrapper. But so will pieces of bread, spoiled vegetables, and other foods we usually throw into the trash. Whether it is plastic, paper, or biodegradable food, we still are littering when we toss it on the ground or onto someone's lawn.

If Kim wants to feed the plants, a compost heap is the place to put the apple core. Too often, we simply toss stuff on the ground, figuring someone will come and pick it up. A look at the sides of some of our highways, sidewalks, beaches, and parks quickly shows how "just one little thing" grows into a huge, unsightly mess. Whether it is shared space inside our house (like our living room) or outside (like a park), everyone has a responsibility to put garbage where it belongs—in the trash!

The Impatient Shopper

*a*fter eating lunch in the school cafeteria, Barrie stops at the student bookstore to buy a notebook she needs for her next-period science class. There is a long line, and she waits impatiently to pay for the book, not wanting to be tardy for class.

Just as it's Barrie's turn at the counter, the cashier says, "I'm sorry, I'm all out of change. Hang on a minute and I'll be right back."

Barrie can't wait any longer, so she goes behind the counter, takes a $2.50 notebook from the shelf, puts $3 down on the counter, and goes to class.

1. What do you think about what Barrie did?

2. Is this stealing?

3. Did Barrie have any other options?

4. If you were the next person in line behind Barrie, what would you do?

{ *Family Discussion* }

This is not stealing, since Barrie did pay for the book. What Barrie did is sometimes called *leading others into temptation.* Even though Barrie was honest and made sure to leave enough money to cover the cost of the notebook, can she be sure that everyone else in line will be as honest as she? By going behind the counter, Barrie is, in effect, saying to others around her, "Help yourself!"

Sometimes we have an obligation to serve as a good role model for others. This may mean not crossing the street against the red light even though we don't see any cars coming, because our action might encourage younger kids to do the same. Barrie also has an obligation to make sure the cashier receives the money for the notebook. There is a chance that if she leaves, someone else might take the money from the counter. In this case, it means that Barrie needs to wait until the cashier returns to get her notebook, or else she should leave for class and come back when she has more time.

Borrowing

*O*n Friday, Rita's friend lent her his crystal collection for the weekend. Rita loves crystals and wanted to look at them under her microscope. She put the crystals in her lunch bag for safekeeping and put them in her bedroom.

On Sunday morning when Rita wanted to look at the crystals, she could not find the bag. "Mom," she yelled frantically, "have you seen a brown lunch bag in my room?"

"Yes, Rita," her mom called back, "I was cleaning yesterday and threw it away. Do you know how many times I've told you not to leave food in your room?"

128

1. What should Rita do?

2. Whose fault is it that the crystals are missing?

3. What else could Rita have done to take better care of the crystals?

4. Have you ever borrowed something from a friend and then misplaced or broken it?

{ Family Discussion }

Rita *and* her mom share some responsibility for this situation. Rita should have carefully labeled the lunch bag so it would not be mistaken for garbage, and her mom should have looked inside the bag before throwing it out. Though Rita did not purposely damage or destroy the crystals, they were her responsibility. If something accidentally happens to an object while we are borrowing it, it is our responsibility to replace the missing item.

We need to take extra care of things we borrow. The person who lends us the item trusts that we will treat it as if it were our own. Maybe a paper bag was not an appropriate container for the crystals. A labeled shoe box or plastic bowl would have been a better choice.

The fact is that now that the crystals are gone, they have to be replaced. Rita is responsible for replacing the crystals. Since Rita's mom bears some responsibility for throwing out the crystals, she should be willing to help pay for replacements.

Trespassing

Mario is adding a third bedroom onto the back of his house. He digs a series of deep holes to sink a foundation for the new addition. While he is away during one weekend, a few of the neighborhood boys come over to poke around the construction. One of them accidentally steps into a hole and badly twists his ankle. His family takes him to the doctor for an X-ray.

When Mario returns, the boy's father goes over to his house and asks him to pay for the cost of the visit to the doctor.

1. Whose fault do you think the accident was?

2. Do you think Mario should pay the doctor's bill?

3. Can you think of some ways in which we keep our homes safe for others?

4. Can you think of a time when you were someplace you didn't belong?

{ Family Discussion }

We have a responsibility to make sure guests and visitors are safe whenever they set foot on our property or enter our homes. The steps leading up to our homes must be safe so others don't slip, our swimming pools must be fenced in so little children can't fall in, and if our dog has a tendency to bite, we must keep him away from visitors.

Here, Mario has dug deep holes in his backyard. He has the responsibility, if he is not going to be around, to cover them up or at least to put up some type of warning around the holes. Yes, the boys were trespassing and shouldn't have been on Mario's property. But Mario has the responsibility to keep his property safe for others, whether they are invited or not. Since the boys and Mario are both at fault, the boy's father and Mario may decide to share the cost of the visit to the doctor.

A Mistake in Your Favor

*M*ai returns home after buying a CD at the music superstore. To her surprise, she finds there are two CDs in her bag, though her receipt shows she was only charged for one. The store clerk must have placed the second CD Mai was considering buying into her bag by accident.

Mai really wanted that second CD but couldn't afford to buy it.

1. If you were Mai, what would you do?

2. If Mai keeps the second CD, is that stealing?

3. Is Mai responsible, even though the mistake was the clerk's?

4. Have you ever accidentally received something that was not yours? What did you do?

{ Family Discussion }

In this case, the lost item belongs not to an individual, but to the music store. It may be hard to feel sorry for the store's loss. But at the end of the month, the cost of missing items may be deducted from the clerks' salaries. If the store is a small one owned by a family, the cost of relatively inexpensive items like missing CDs adds up very quickly. When lots of items are missing or stolen from stores, the stores must raise prices to make up for the money. So even though Mai has only one extra CD, it will cost the store— and the customers—more money in the long run if she does not return the CD. If you don't pay for something, even if you didn't take it on purpose, it still does not belong to you.

"It's My Room!"

Jeffrey loves to skateboard, and he collects stickers from the companies that make boards. One day after school while listening to music, he decides to do a little room redecorating. He carefully places the stickers on the wall across from his bed. "Cool," he thinks, admiring his work. "Now my room really looks good."

Just then, his mom comes in and gasps, "Jeffrey, what is going on in here? These stickers will be impossible to get off your wall. Why did you do this? How could you have ruined your room like this?"

"Mom, this is *my* room!" says Jeffrey. "I can do anything I want to in here. What's the big deal? I'll keep my door shut so you won't have to see it."

1. What do you think about this situation?

2. Who is responsible for Jeffrey's room?

3. Is there any way Jeffrey and his mom could figure out a way to compromise?

{ *Family Discussion* }

Perhaps Jeffrey's mom is overreacting. How he decorates his room should not be that important. After all, it will not affect his behavior or his grades. Yet, this is part of his family's home. Stickers on the wall could destroy the paint when they are removed. Perhaps his mom felt that some of the stickers were inappropriate.

On the other hand, the stickers are a way for Jeffrey to express himself. It is important to find ways of self-expression, but these must not cause harm to others or their property. Jeffrey's mom did not make the house rules clear and Jeffrey didn't ask before putting up his stickers. If they had talked about it, a compromise could have been reached. For instance, she could have bought Jeffrey a bulletin board on which to put his stickers. Since the stickers are already up, his mom might allow him to keep the stickers on the wall, if Jeffrey agrees to repaint his wall when the stickers come down.

Dress Codes

"*H*urry up, dear," says Tina's mother. "You're going to be late for school!"

Tina slips on a pair of jeans, pulls a tank top over her head, and races out of the house to reach the corner before the school bus arrives.

As Tina enters her English class, her teacher looks up from the desk and immediately tells her that the tank top she is wearing is inappropriate and violates the school's dress code. "Does it really matter what I'm wearing?" asks Tina. "It's not like it affects my grades or anything!"

Tina's English teacher sends her to the principal's office.

1. Do you think it matters how students dress at school?

2. Do you think it's fair that schools have codes about what you can and can't wear?

3. Is there a connection between how kids at your school dress and the grades they get?

{ Family Discussion }

There are reasons why there are dress codes. Some schools have dress codes to help students avoid the pressure of having to buy trendy shoes, pants, or tops. Often the most popular styles of clothing are expensive, and many students who can't afford to buy these kinds of clothes may be shunned by others because they're not dressed in style. This kind of environment makes it hard for kids to learn.

Sometimes dress codes are required because of gangs: gang clothing separates students into different groups that are pitted against each other. Students not in a gang who mistakenly wear gang garb might find themselves in physical danger.

Some schools have dress codes because they find that some clothes are too sexually suggestive, and they want the students' focus to be on the blackboard, not on someone else's body! The fact is, we tend to judge people too often by how they look, regardless of what type of person they are inside. While Tina is at school, she needs to follow the school's rules; outside of school (assuming her parents approve), she can dress as she wants.

The X-rated Book

*N*ed's mom is putting away his laundry. She opens the drawer to put Ned's T-shirts away and notices a paperback book tucked in the corner. The subject of the book is not appropriate for younger readers, and Ned's mom is shocked at the half-nude photos on the cover. After all, Ned is only twelve years old.

She puts the book back in the drawer and closes it.

1. Should Ned's mom talk to him about the book?

2. Would the situation be different if Ned's mom found a knife or a pack of cigarettes in his drawer?

3. Isn't Ned old enough to decide what to read?

{ *Family Discussion* }

All families have rules about privacy, such as: don't walk into the bathroom if someone else is in there; don't go in sibling's drawers without their permission; and don't enter mom and dad's room when the door is shut. In Ned's case, perhaps his mom can give Ned the responsibility of putting away his own laundry.

Privacy is important. Everyone needs some time to be by themselves. People need to feel confident that their possessions will not be touched or looked at by others without permission. As long as privacy does not hurt other people or serve as a way to hurt ourselves, it should be respected. Ned's mom should not say anything to Ned about the book that she found, because it is a private matter and doesn't hurt anyone. She could, however, set up a time to talk as a family about general sexual issues. This way, she can respect Ned's privacy and address her own concerns.

The Second Hole

*B*rooke comes home from school, drops her backpack on the kitchen counter, and announces to her mother that she wants to get a second hole pierced in each ear. Her mom gives her a look of concern and says, "When you got your ears pierced last year, you never mentioned wanting more than one hole!"

"You know, Mom," Brooke says, "you have pierced ears. What's the difference if I add an extra hole to each ear?" Brooke's mom is now looking more concerned. She says nothing, but is shaking her head no. "It's my body and I can do what I want with it!" Brooke shouts. "What do you care anyway? My hair covers my ears! How does it hurt you?"

1. Do you see anything wrong with what Brooke is requesting?

2. What would you do if you were Brooke's mom?

3. How much say should parents have in what their children choose to wear or do to their body?

4. Do you think it would make a difference if Brooke wanted to get a tattoo?

{ *Family Discussion* }

Parents have the task of helping their children make wise choices as they are growing up. The job of a parent is to teach a child how to problem-solve. By dressing in a certain way, Brooke is giving a message to others about herself and about her family. Her mother may feel a second hole is inappropriate for a girl Brooke's age, and she wants Brooke to reflect her family's values.

On the other hand, Brooke makes a couple of good points. It is her body, and her hair will cover her ears. She should be able to make decisions about her own body. Brooke's mother has said she is too young for a second pair of holes. Brooke could ask at what age would a second hole be okay. Brooke and her mother could agree upon a time in the not-so-distant future when Brooke could get her ears pierced again.

An Unwelcome Hug

*I*t is Mona's senior year of high school, and she is given the privilege of being a teacher's assistant in Mr. Clampton's chemistry lab. Mona is thrilled with the job, and Mr. Clampton seems very happy with her work.

After class on Thursday, Mr. Clampton puts his arms around Mona and gives her a long hug. Holding her tightly, he says, "I don't know what I'd do without you!"

Mona leaves the lab feeling confused and upset. She likes Mr. Clampton, and she loved hearing his praise, but the hug made her uncomfortable.

1. If you were Mona, what would you do?

2. If you decided to tell someone about how Mr. Clampton made you feel, who would you tell?

3. Is it ever okay for a teacher to hug a student?

4. Have you ever been in a situation where someone's words or actions towards you made you feel uncomfortable?

{ Family Discussion }

Unwelcome touching is not okay. It doesn't matter if Mr. Clampton was acting friendly, teasing, or very serious. The fact is that he touched Mona in a way that made her feel uncomfortable. Adults with authority have a special responsibility to act appropriately and avoid unwelcome touching. A teacher with a student, a boss with his or her employee, or a coach with a team member all have to respect and not abuse their positions of power. Because it has taken place between an adult and a minor, Mona's situation is even more serious.

Sometimes people who receive unwelcome touching are reluctant to report what has happened. Some feel they may have encouraged it, and think it is their fault. Others don't want the person who touched them to get in trouble. But no one has the right to touch our body without our permission.

Though it may be difficult, it is important for Mona to share what happened with someone she trusts. If she is too embarrassed or shy to speak to Mr. Clampton, she might talk with her parents, a school counselor, or a friend. By taking action and telling someone about it, Mona can help ensure that this won't happen to others.

About the Authors

JEFFREY A. MARX is rabbi of Sha'arei Am in Santa Monica, California, where he is a family counselor, teacher, and storyteller. He is trained as a family mediator and has been involved in family education for the past thirteen years. He is the father of Sarah, Jonathan, and Benjamin.

JULES PORTER

RISA MUNITZ GRUBERGER is the Associate Director of the Whizin Institute for Jewish Family Life in Los Angeles. Through workshops, in-service training, lectures, and published materials, Risa has reached hundreds of families, teachers, and graduate students with her innovative programs and ideas for parents and children. She lives in Los Angeles with her husband, Don, and two children, Brittney and Michael.